HULL'S

SURRENDER OF DETROIT.

By BENSON J. LOSSING, LL.D.

REPRINTED, WITH ADDITIONS, FROM "POTTER'S AMERICAN MONTHLY," AUGUST, 1875.

PHILADELPHIA:
JOHN E. POTTER AND COMPANY,
No. 617 SANSOM STREET.

HULL'S

SURRENDER OF DETROIT.

By BENSON J. LOSSING, LL.D.

REPRINTED, WITH ADDITIONS, FROM "POTTER'S AMERICAN MONTHLY,"
AUGUST, 1875.

PHILADELPHIA:
JOHN E. POTTER AND COMPANY,
No. 617 SANSOM STREET.

The article by Dr. Lossing, here reprinted by his consent and that of his publishers, first appeared in "Potter's American Monthly Magazine," August, 1875, No. 44. A few passages, not bearing on the Surrender of Detroit, have been omitted; and a few notes referring to the authorities, added.

HULL'S

SURRENDER OF DETROIT.

THE name of William Hull holds a conspicuous place in the annals of our country—conspicuous for gallant deeds and patient suffering under false accusations. I do not propose to give in this paper a biography of this citizen; only outline pictures of the more salient points in the history of his life, from his birth in Derby, a village on the Housatonic River, in Connecticut, in 1753, until his death in Newton, Massachusetts, in 1825. He labored gallantly in the camp and in the field whenever opportunity offered, and he suffered the stings of unjust public reproach many years, that were set in motion by a few selfish, ambitious or ignorant men, who misled the judgment of the nation. These even secured the ear of History, and that misled judgment obscured her vision, and to this day she has taught the world (with few exceptions) untruthful stories about the character and career of an American citizen who deserves the love and veneration of his countrymen for his brave and generous deeds. It is a pleasant task for me to recall from the obscurity of the past a vindication of the patriot who made his dwelling-house at Newton one of the conspicuous Historic Buildings of America.

After his graduation at Yale College young Hull studied divinity a year, to fit him for the Christian ministry, in compliance with the wishes of his parents. He could not conscientiously make the profession of a clergyman his life pursuit, and he entered the Law School at Litchfield, Connecticut. In 1775 he was admitted to the Bar, and had just entered upon its practice when the War for Independence broke out. He had taken an active part in the Revolutionary movements. One evening his father, returning from a public meeting of the citizens of Derby, said, "William, who do you suppose has been elected captain of the company that has been raised in this town?" William named several, when his father surprised him by saying, "It is you." He accepted the honors and duties of his position, closed the doors of his law-office, and entered upon military duties under Colonel Webb. At about the same time Hull's father died, and left his considerable estate to his widow and children. William refused to receive any part of it, saying, "I only want my sword and my uniform." A few days afterward he was on his way with his company to join Washington at Cambridge. From that time until the close of hostilities he was an active and skillful soldier. Dorchester Heights, White Plains, Trenton and Princeton witnessed the achievements that won for him the commission of major. At Ticonderoga, Stillwater, Saratoga, Monmouth and Stony Point his skill and valor won for him the commission of lieutenant-colonel; and when he assisted in the capture of Cornwallis, late in 1781, he held the commission of colonel.

Early in 1781, after having served about six years in the army without asking for a furlough, he obtained leave of absence to complete a conquest and take possession of the prize won by his valor in another field. He repaired to Boston in February, 1781, and soon afterward was married to Sarah, only daughter of Judge Fuller, of Newton, Massachusetts. Of that victory and its results the veteran soldier wrote from the home of his bride, the Hull mansion, at Newton, in 1822: "It was a reward for all the toils and dangers which, for six years, I had encountered. It has continued for nearly forty years, and my beloved companion has not only sailed with me down the stream of life, enjoying its prosperous gales, but has steadily and affectionately supported me in gloomy periods, as well as in the last trying storm which, by faith in an overruling Providence, I have met and borne in all its fury."

I will pass on with only brief mention of the principal events in the life of Colonel Hull, after his marriage, to his appointment as Governor of the Territory of Michigan.

When the army of the Revolution was about to be disbanded, and Washington and a few troops entered the city of New York on the day when the British left it, Colonel Hull was selected to lead the military escort of the Commander-in-Chief on that occasion, and was with him until his departure for Annapolis to resign his commission. In 1786 Hull retired from the army, and for several years practiced law in Newton with marked success. He soon became a leading man there, representing his district in the Massachusetts Legislature, and being made a major-general of militia. In Shay's rebellion he commanded one wing of Lincoln's forces. Pushing on to the camp of the insurgents in spite of a violent snow-storm, he surprised and dispersed them. In 1793 he was sent by the government of the United States to treat with the Indians in Canada; and five years afterward he went to Europe. After his return he was appointed Judge of the Court of Common Pleas of Massachusetts.

President Jefferson appointed General Hull Governor of the Territory of Michigan* in 1805, which office he held until 1812.

* The white inhabitants of Michigan in 1811 were 4,860 in number, four-fifths of whom were French. With the exception of a small strip of land on the river and lake, all the present State of Michigan was occupied by Indians—

Detroit, a small struggling village on the west side of the Detroit River, was the capital of his domain, and was inhabited chiefly by French Canadians. There he built a house for his family, and invested a large portion of his fortune in real estate. During the winter and spring of 1812 he was in Washington City, where he listened with anxiety to the debates in Congress on the subject of a declaration of war against Great Britain, for he feared that in the event of such a declaration the government would be in favor of an immediate invasion of Canada. Hull well knew the perils to his own Territory which such an invasion would involve, and always gave his voice against it. He well knew what pains the British authorities in Canada had taken, by presents of firearms and other things, to induce the Indian tribes of the Northwest to become their allies.* He well knew how successful the British had been in their diplomacy to that end, and he knew that the moment American troops should cross the Detroit River into Canada, there was danger of an invasion of Michigan, and the complete desolation of the Territory. Without a fleet on Lake Erie,† of which the British were masters, it would be almost impossible to defend Michigan, much less to invade Canada with success by such a force as might be raised in that region.

President Madison listened to Hull's advice to some extent, but he was overruled by others having more force than himself. He persuaded Governor Hull to accept the office of brigadier-general in the regular army, made a requisition upon Governor Meigs, of

---

Pottawattomies, Miamis, Wyandots, Chippewas, Winnebagoes and Ottawas.—"*Military and Civil Life of General Hull.*" *New York: D. Appleton & Co., 1848*, page 307.

* See "*Civil and Military Life of General Hull,*" page 310.

† In three separate memorials addressed to the War Department in April, 1809, June, 1811, and March, 1812, General Hull had urged the necessity of a fleet on Lake Erie. Again, after his appointment as brigadier-general, he urged the same thing in a memorial to the President.—"*Military and Civil Life,*" etc., pages 327–413.

Ohio, for a detachment of twelve hundred militia to be disciplined, and prepared to march instantly for Detroit when they should be called for. Hull accepted the commission of brigadier-general only that he might more efficiently protect his domain against the savages.* He returned to Detroit, resolved to do whatever his country should demand of him, but with a strong hope that war would be averted.

Hull's hopes were disappointed, for in June following, our government formally declared war against Great Britain. Governor Meigs, meanwhile, had gathered and disciplined the militia of Ohio† with great alacrity, and late in May he had placed them under the command of Hull in an open field near Dayton. The veteran soldier, then about sixty years of age, made a patriotic speech to them, when they all moved forward cheerfully toward Detroit, up the valley of the Miami or Maumee River. As he advanced, Hull had sure indications of Indian hostilities. Tecumtha was the ally of the British, and his authority was almost supreme over a vast region, and over many savages.

On the 24th of June, six days after war had been declared, Hull received a despatch from the War Department, directing him to hasten with his troops to Detroit, and there await further orders. A little more than a week later, when he was at Frenchtown (now

---

* See "*Military and Civil Life*," etc., page 326.

† The Ohio volunteers were militia just called into the field, and were deficient in discipline. Lieutenant Bacon, of the Fourth United States Infantry, testified at the court-martial as follows: "Generally speaking, the Ohio volunteers and militia were insubordinate. One evening, at Urbana, I saw a multitude and heard a noise, and was informed that a company of Ohio volunteers were riding one of their officers on a rail. Witness thinks he saw one hundred of the Ohio militia who refused to cross into Canada."—*Forbes's* "*Report of the Court-Martial*," page 124.

The arms and equipments of these troops were unfit for service; the men were without blankets, clothing or ammunition, and the government had made no provision for either.—"*Memoirs of the Campaign of 1812*," *by William Hull. True & Greene, Boston, 1824*, page 34.

Monroe, Michigan), he received another despatch, informing him of the declaration of war.* The British authorities in Canada had received earlier intelligence of the event, and acted accordingly. Before Hull received the second despatch, he had hired a schooner for the conveyance of his heavy baggage, intrenching tools, etc., to Detroit, so that he might relieve his wearied pack-horses. This vessel sailed from the site of Toledo on the day before he received the news of the declaration of war. She was captured by an armed vessel sent out from Malden. By mistake his private papers containing the muster-rolls of his army, and other information which he did not wish the enemy to possess, had been placed on board of the schooner.

When the wearied troops reached Detroit, Hull rested and awaited orders, according to his instructions. The British were constructing fortifications on the opposite side of the river that might endanger Detroit, and Hull's officers, most of them ardent young men, were impatient to invade Canada and drive off the fort-builders. They urged the General to do so, when he replied, "I have no authority to invade Canada." They insisted that it was his duty to do so, under the circumstances. He replied firmly, "While I have the command I will obey the orders of my government. I will not cross over until I hear from Washington." The young officers were much irritated, and felt rebellious. That night a despatch was received from the Secretary of War, directing Hull "to commence operations immediately." This relieved the General from perplexity and satisfied his officers.

With about sixteen hundred effective men,† Hull now crossed

---

* See Hull's "*Memoirs*," as above, page 35; also, "*Armstrong's Notices of the War of 1812*," pages 47, 48.

† Major Jessup, Brigade-Major of the army, testified at the court-martial that Hull crossed into Canada with sixteen or eighteen hundred men. The estimate of his force made by General Hull himself was fourteen hundred.—*Forbes's "Report of the Court-Martial*," page 42.

the Detroit River, raised the American standard, and issued a stirring proclamation to the inhabitants of Canada, in which assurance was given that the peaceful and quiet dwellers should be secure in person and property, but no quarters would be given to any who should be found fighting side by side with the Indians. A copy of that proclamation, with an account of his movements, was sent by Hull to the Secretary of War. The latter wrote to the General, "Your operations are approved by the government." When disaster followed, this approval was concealed, and histories for more than fifty years declared that the invasion was unauthorized. The American Commissioners at the Treaty of Ghent, misled, made the same declaration.

Hull's invasion of Canada was a failure. His excessive caution won for him the dislike, the injurious suspicions, and the contempt of his young and impatient officers, who wished to march immediately upon Fort Malden, an important British post eighteen miles below Detroit. At about the same time news came from the far north, that the American fort at Mackinaw had been captured by a force of British and Indians, and that the savage hosts in that region were about to go upon the war-path into Michigan. Hull knew better than his young officers the perils that menaced his army, and the necessity for its preservation for the protection of the inhabitants of his Territory. They could not know the anxiety that produced his caution, and they charged the General (secretly at first, and then quite openly) with imbecility, cowardice, and even treason. But he remained dutiful to his convictions of right; and early in August he ordered his little army to abandon the invasion of Canada and recross the river.

Meanwhile Major-General Brock had been sent to the western frontier of Canada with a few British regulars and a militia force.*

---

* General Brock's own account of his force was, whites, 730 men; Indians, 600; 1,330 in all; but he seems to have underrated his own force, for in his

He cast up intrenchments opposite Detroit, and on the 15th of August he sent a summons to Hull, demanding an immediate surrender of his troops, fort, town, and Territory. The summons was accompanied by a covert threat to let loose the savages upon the Americans.

Hull was now moved by conflicting emotions. His pride of character, his patriotism, and his desire to satisfy his officers bade him fight, his tender regard for his troops and the inhabitants of the town bade him surrender.* He obeyed the former impulse at

---

biography it is stated that one thousand Indians, under Tecumseh, met him in council at Amherstburg, and all expressed their determination to fight on his side.—"*Military and Civil Life*," etc., page 362.

General Brock had also all the sailors and marines of his naval force, then lying in the Detroit River, and a detachment of British troops under Major Chambers, which came from Niagara to reinforce him, amounting to several hundred men.—*Hull's* "*Memoirs*," page 115.

From these two sources at least five hundred men must have been added to his force, which would therefore be—

Regulars and Canadian militia	730
Major Chambers's reinforcement, with sailors and marines from the fleet	500
Indians	1000
	2230 men.

The testimony of Major Snelling, a swift witness for the prosecution, as to the numbers of the enemy, was so given that it is difficult to say whether he made them to be 750 men or 2,250. It may be interpreted either way.—*Forbes's* "*Report of Court-Martial*," page 40.

Robert Wallace, of Kentucky, who was one of General Hull's aids during the campaign, wrote an interesting account of it for a Western newspaper, in which he stated that "the British regulars and Canadians were about three thousand men; but the numbers of Indians could not have been known by Brock himself. In addition to Tecumseh's band and the Wyandots, they had gathered in from all the regions of the Northern lakes—a countless number." Mr. Wallace states that his summons as a witness did not reach him in season to allow him to give evidence at the trial—which was unfortunate for General Hull.—"*Civil and Military Life of William Hull*," page 443.

* Beside the inhabitants of the town, there were, as we have seen, a large number of white persons scattered through the Territory of Michigan, who would have been massacred by the Indians as soon as fighting began.

first, and defied Brock. The latter opened a severe cannonade on the fort and town. British troops and Indian warriors were sent across the river to attack the Americans. Battle lines were formed, and the American soldiers, confident of victory, were eager, it is said, to measure strength with the foe. Hull did not share with his troops the expectation of victory. On the contrary, he expected defeat, and just as a conflict was about to begin, the General ordered his men to retreat into the fort. They were astounded, bewildered, and exasperated, but obeyed.

Impressed by a sense of imminent danger to the lives of his soldiery and the inhabitants of the town from the fierce cruelty of an overwhelming number of savages, the General, without consulting any of his officers, now ordered a white flag to be unfurled over the fort, when the firing ceased. Very soon afterwards the fort was surrendered by Hull, with the troops, the town, and the Territory. The officers and soldiers were greatly excited. The act was so sudden that they could hardly believe their senses. The General had not even suggested the possibility of a surrender. Not a gun had been fired against the enemy; not an effort had been made to stay his course. The troops (so testified the officers) felt that they had been betrayed. Nothing but respect for gray hai s and veneration for a soldier of the Revolution saved Hull from personal violence for a moment. The soldiers* were paroled and sent home; the General and the other officers were

---

* General Hull's own estimate of his force at the time of the surrender was . . . . 800 men.
The average of Major Jessup's two estimates . . . . 850 "
Colonel Cass's statement in his letter of September 10th . 1060 "
General Brock's statement of the number captured . . 2500 "
Colonel Cass was absent at the time of the surrender, and derived his information from others. General Brock made the number captured one thousand greater than any number General Hull had under his command during the campaign. The statement of the Brigade-Major, Jessup, is probably reliable.

taken as captives to Montreal, where they were soon exchanged or otherwise released.

At Fort George, on the Niagara River, Hull wrote a report of recent proceedings to the Secretary of War, but was not permitted to send it until he reached Montreal. In that report he generously took all the responsibility of the act of surrender upon himself. "I well knew the responsibility of the measure," he wrote, "and take the whole of it on myself. It was dictated by a sense of duty, and a full conviction of its expediency. The bands of savages which had then joined the British force were numerous beyond example. Their numbers have since increased; and the history of the barbarians of the north of Europe does not furnish examples of more greedy violence than these savages have exhibited. A large portion of the brave and gallant officers and men I command would cheerfully have contested until the last cartridge had been expended and bayonets worn to the sockets. I could not consent to the useless sacrifice of such brave men when I knew it was impossible for me to sustain my situation. It was impossible, in the nature of things, that an army could have been furnished with the necessary supplies of provisions, military stores, clothing, and comforts for the sick, or pack-horses, through a wilderness of two hundred miles, filled with hostile savages.* It was impossible, Sir, that this little army, worn down by fatigue, by sickness, by wounds, and deaths, could have supported itself not only against the collected force of all the northern Indians, but against the united strength of Upper Canada, whose population consists of more than twenty times the number contained in the Territory of Michigan, aided by the principal part of the regular forces of the

* By the evidence of Baird, the contractor for the supply of the army at Detroit, it appears that on the day of the surrender, the provisions were almost exhausted, and two expeditions sent out to bring in supplies had been defeated by the Indians.—*Hull's "Memoirs,"* page 77.

province, and the wealth and influence of the Northwest and other trading establishments among the Indians, who have in their employment more than two thousand men."*

In the meantime a few troops under Colonel McArthur, who had not arrived at Detroit, had been included in the surrender and parole. Colonel Cass immediately started for Washington City to communicate a history of the affair to the government. It was made in writing, and exhibited much warmth of feeling against General Hull. It was made up of a few *facts* and many expressions of *opinion.* "To see the whole of our men flushed with a hope of victory," Cass wrote, "eagerly awaiting the approaching contest—to see them afterwards dispirited, hopeless, and desponding, at least five hundred shedding tears because they were not allowed to meet their country's foe and to fight their country's battles, excited sensations which no American has ever before had cause to feel, and which, I trust in God, will never again be felt while our men remain to defend the standard of the Union . . . Confident I am that, had the courage and conduct of the General been equal to the spirit and zeal of the troops, the event would have been as brilliant and successful as it is disastrous and dishonorable."†

* The fact which made the surrender of Hull necessary, was that his communications were entirely cut off, and both attempts to restore them had failed. Food and ammunition were nearly gone—the army was cut off from its base, and fell, as a matter of course. In the same way, during our Civil War, Charleston, which had successfully resisted the most powerful assaults from the army and fleet of the Union, fell without a blow as soon as Sherman had cut its railroad communications.

† Mr. Silliman, of Zanesville, Ohio, brother-in-law of Colonel Cass, testified, on the trial, that on the 12th of August, four days before the surrender, Cass wrote to him in these terms: "Our situation is critical. Men and provisons are necessary for our existence. I wish you to hasten the march of troops from your parts. Is there nothing to be done on the lake to make a diversion in our favor? As bad as you may think of our situation, it is still worse than you believe."—*Forbes's "Report of the Trial,"* page 135. Compare this with his statements after the surrender.

This sensational history was scattered broadcast over the country by the newspapers, and excited intense indignation against the unfortunate General in the public mind. It was welcomed by Dr. Eustis, the Secretary of War, and General Dearborn, the Commander-in-Chief, as a foil to the just censure which they would have received for remissness in official duty had the whole truth been known; how the Secretary omitted to inform Hull of the declaration of war until it was known in Canada, and even in the wilderness near Mackinaw; and how Dearborn had failed to communicate to Hull the fact that he had agreed to an armistice which relieved Brock from duty on the Niagara frontier, and allowed him to hasten to the western frontier of Canada. Hull was made the scapegoat of these officers, and they allowed him to suffer for their own sins. He was abused by almost everybody and everywhere, without stint, and the most impossible stories were told and believed about his being bribed by the British to surrender. The absurd story was put afloat and actually credited that a wagon-load of "British gold" had been taken to his house at Newton, whither he had retired to the shelter of domestic life from the storm of vituperation, after his return from captivity in September.

The well-informed government and the ill-informed people joined in the pursuit of General Hull with the lash of bitter calumny; the former with the selfish intention to shield itself from reproach, and the latter impelled by a righteous indignation against one whom they regarded as an almost unpardonable sinner. The people had been made to believe by the politicians of the war party that Canada might be very easily conquered by a small American force, and public expectation ran high, when news came in that our flag had been unfurled upon its soil. But men of more wisdom and experience had formed contrary opinions. General Harrison had seen, from the beginning, the danger of such an invasion as that undertaken by Hull. And when he heard of the fall of Mackinaw, he regarded it as the forerunner of the capture of Chicago and Detroit. This opinion he expressed in a letter written on the 6th of August. On the 10th he again wrote to the Secretary of War, saying: "I greatly fear that the capture of Mackinaw will give such *éclat* to the British and Indians that the Northern Tribes will pour down in swarms upon Detroit, oblige General Hull to act on the defensive, and meet and perhaps overpower the convoys and reinforcements which may be sent to him." This is precisely what happened when Van Horne, with a detachment, went to meet a convoy of supplies from Ohio. Harrison continues: "It appears to me, indeed, highly probable that the large detachment which is now destined for his (Hull's) relief, under Colonel Wells, will have to fight its way. I greatly rely on the valor of those troops, but it is possible that the event may be adverse to us, and if it is, *Detroit must fall*, and with it every hope of reëstablishing our affairs in that quarter until the next year.

Soon after General Hull returned to his home in Newton he was placed under arrest, and the government preferred grave charges against him. A court-martial assembled at Philadelphia late in February, 1813, with General Wade Hampton as President, and A. J. Dallas as Judge-Advocate. Hull, who was anxious for an investigation, appeared with alacrity before the court; but the President of the United States dissolved the court before it had entered upon its business, without giving a reason for the act. It was almost a year before another court-martial was convened at Albany, with General Dearborn as President, assisted by three brigadier-generals, four colonels and five lieutenant-colonels. These were Generals Bloomfield, Parker and Covington; Colonels Fenwick, Carberry, Little and Irvine; and Lieutenant-Colonels Dennis, Connor, Davis, Scott and Stewart. Mr. Dallas was again the Judge-Advocate, and the government employed able counsel to assist him.

A majority of the members of this court were young men recently promoted to their respective offices. Some of them had served as aids to General Dearborn, and had been introduced into the army by his patronage. General Hull might, with great propriety, have objected to the composition of the court, for he blamed General Dearborn for his negligence, and his own acquittal would condemn that officer. But he was anxious for an investigation, and he waived all feeling. The court opened business on the 3d of January, 1814.

General Hull was charged with *Treason, Cowardice, and Neglect of duty and unofficerlike conduct from the 9th of April to August* 16, 1812. The specifications under the charge of *Treason* were: (1.) Hiring the vessel to transport his sick men and baggage from the Miami (at Toledo) to Detroit; (2.) Not attacking the enemy's fort at Malden, and retreating to Detroit; (3.) Not strengthening the fort at Detroit, and surrendering. The specifications under the charge of *Cowardice* were: (1.) Not attacking Malden, and retreating to Detroit; (2.) Appearance of alarm during the cannonade; (3.) Appearance of alarm on the day of the surrender; (4.) Surrender of Detroit. The specifications under the third charge were similar to those under the second.

This trial, in most of its aspects, was a remarkable and most disgraceful one, and no sensible man can read the record of it without a conviction that General Hull was offered a sacrifice to appease public indignation, and to the necessity of preserving the Administration from disgrace and contempt. The court was evidently constituted for this end. The President of the court, who was the Commander-in-Chief of the armies, was deeply interested in the conviction of General Hull. He had made a serious and (for Hull) a fatal blunder in concluding an armistice with Sir George Prevost without including the Army of the Northwest, or even advising its commander of the omission. If Hull should be acquitted, the

President of the court might be compelled to appear before a similar tribunal on a charge of neglect of duty. It is a significant fact to be remembered that the President was called from very important military duties at that time, to preside over a trial that lasted eighty days, when there were other peers of the accused not nearly as much engaged as the Commander-in-Chief. The principal witnesses against the accused were allowed extraordinary latitude. They were permitted to give their *opinions* concerning military movements, which were admitted as evidence; a thing unheard of in a court, excepting in the case of medical or other experts. Chiefly upon such kind of testimony the unfortunate General was condemned. Some militia officers who had never been under fire, testified that because of the peculiar appearance of the General's face during the cannonade of the fort it was their opinion that he was moved by fear; whilst others, who had been in battle, attributed his appearance to the real cause—exhausting fatigue of mind and body, for neither had enjoyed any rest scarcely for several days and nights.

The charge of treason was withdrawn at the beginning of the trial, in a manner most injurious to the accused, namely, that the court had no jurisdiction; but when the trial was over, they saw the necessity of saying, in their verdict: "The evidence on the subject having been publicly given, the court deem it proper, in justice to the accused, to say that they do not believe, from anything that has appeared before them, that General Hull has committed treason against the United States." Why this show of "ju tice to the accused?" The reason is obvious. The principal fact on which the charge of treason was based was the sending of the baggage, intrenching tools, and sick, by water past a British fort after war was declared. Because of the neglect of the Secretary of War to send an early notice to Hull of that declaration, the latter was ignorant of the important act until after his schooner had sailed. He might have received the notice some days before she sailed, had the Secretary not been remiss in his duty. That fact, and the proof which appeared that the British at Malden had received a notice of the declaration of war before Hull's vessel sailed, in a letter franked by the Secretary of the Treasury (in consequence of which the British were enabled to send an armed vessel out of Malden to capture Hull's schooner), were likely to be damaging to the Administration; so the court, more ready to serve the government than to do justice, dismissed the charge of treason, and made a forced acknowledgment of the General's innocence of that crime. But upon the strength of the extraordinary testimony alluded to, they found the veteran soldier guilty of the second and third charges, and sentenced him to be shot dead! On account of his Revolutionary services, as the court alleged, they earnestly recommended him to the mercy of the President. Madison approved the sentence, but pardoned the alleged offender. By this act Justice and Mercy, in the public estimation, were satisfied; the Administration was absolved from its sins by sacrificing upon the altar of its selfishness the character (which was to him dearer than life) of the innocent victim, and History was allowed to unconsciously defile her pen by writing falsely of the immolated patriot. What a relief to the Administration from crushing responsibility was this unjust sentence! The Secretary of War, conscious of his own errors, expected to feel the public wrath, and had written to General Dearborn: "Fortunately for you, the want of success which has attended the campaign will be attributed to the Secretary of War."

General Hull lived under a dark cloud of unmerited reproach, and was compelled to keep silent for the want of facts to establish his innocence. His papers were burned while on their way from Detroit to Buffalo, after the surrender; and during two Administrations he was denied the privilege of obtaining copies of papers in the War Department at Washington that might vindicate his character. When John C. Calhoun became Secretary of War, he generously gave Hull permission to copy any paper he wished. With the material so obtained, the General began the preparation of a vindication, which was published in a series of letters in a Boston newspaper (*American Statesman*) in 1824, when he was past three-score-and-ten years of age. He lived long enough after publishing that vindication to perceive unmistakable signs of sympathy in the partially disabused public mind, which prophesied of future awards of justice. In 1825 the citizens of Boston testified their respect for him by giving him a public dinner.

In the darkest hours of his adversity General Hull enjoyed the society of generous friends outside of his loving family circle, who thoroughly believed in him. He was in continual correspondence with his old and sympathizing companions-in-arms; and men of high degree in social life were sometimes his guests. Lafayette visited him when that distinguished Frenchman was the nation's guest fifty years ago.

In judging the conduct of General Hull at Detroit, we must remember that he was far down the western slope of life at the time of his surrender, when men are very cautious, and when they are more apt to counsel than to act. The perils and fatigues of the march from Dayton to Detroit had affected him, and the anxieties arising from his responsibilities bore heavily upon his judgment. These difficulties his young, vigorous, ambitious and daring officers could not understand; and while they were cursing him, they should have been kindly cherishing him. When he could perceive no alternative but surrender or destruction—destruction to his army and the old men, women and children who had taken refuge in Detroit from the fury of the savages—he bravely determined to choose the most courageous and humane course; so he faced the taunts of his soldiers and the expected scorn of his countrymen, rather than fill the beautiful land of the Ohio and the young settlements of Michigan with mourning. To one of his aids he said: "You return to your family without a stain; as for myself I have sacrificed a reputation dearer to me than life, but I have saved the inhabitants of Detroit, and my heart approves the act."

The conception of the campaign against Canada was a huge blunder. Hull saw it and protested against it. The failure to put in vigorous motion for his support auxiliary and coöperative forces was criminal neglect. When the result was found to be a failure and humiliation, the Administration perceived it and sought a refuge. Public indignation must be appeased; the lightning of the public wrath must be averted. I repeat it—General Hull was made the chosen victim for the peace-offering—the sin-bearing scapegoat—and on his head the fiery thunderbolts were hurled. The case of General Hull illustrates the force of Shakspeare's words:

> "'Tis strange how many unimagined charges
> Can swarm upon a man when once the lid
> Of the Pandora box of contumely
> Is opened o'er his head."

www.ingramcontent.com/pod-product-compliance
Lightning Source LLC
LaVergne TN
LVHW011146110826
845150LV00008B/2543
* 9 7 8 1 4 1 8 1 9 1 7 8 8 *